Sacred Grounds

poems by

Cooper Young

Finishing Line Press
Georgetown, Kentucky

Sacred Grounds

Copyright © 2020 by Cooper Young
ISBN 978-1-64662-190-3 First Edition
All rights reserved under International and Pan-American Copyright Conventions. No part of this book may be reproduced in any manner whatsoever without written permission from the publisher, except in the case of brief quotations embodied in critical articles and reviews.

ACKNOWLEDGMENTS

"A Heron in the Garden" and "English Learning: Poetry" originally appeared in *Miramar*.
"Behind the Glass" was first published in *Nassau Literary Review*.
"The Home of Wild Animals" and "Where Owls Won't Fly" originally appeared in *The Wayfarer*.

"Where Owls Won't Fly" was the co-winner of the Morris W. Croll Poetry Prize awarded by Princeton University's Department of English, 2018.

I would like to express my immense gratitude to the Lewis Center for the Arts at Princeton University, and especially to the Adam family, whose generous support made this project a reality.

Publisher: Leah Maines
Editor: Christen Kincaid
Cover Art: Cooper Young
Author Photo: Jake Young
Cover Design: Elizabeth Maines McCleavy

Printed in the USA on acid-free paper.
Order online: www.finishinglinepress.com
　　　　　also available on amazon.com

Author inquiries and mail orders:
Finishing Line Press
P. O. Box 1626
Georgetown, Kentucky 40324
U. S. A.

Table of Contents

Posture 1

Waiting for Rain to Pass in Bashō's Hut............................. 2

Riding the No. 5 to the Mountains..................................... 3

An Evening Before the Rain.. 4

A Universal Accent... 5

Conversations by the Kamo River...................................... 6

Daisen-In: The Academy of the Great Immortals............. 7

The Home of Wild Animals 8

A Home to Rest In.. 9

A Crowd Around the Shrine... 10

A Heron in the Garden 11

Where Owls Won't Fly 12

Behind the Glass.. 13

Hunt 14

Poison.. 15

Child's Play 16

English Learning: Poetry... 17

Aged Wine... 18

One More Mile... 19

The Kamo River 20

August 21

Naked 22

No Other Life... 23

For my family

Posture
>   *June 15, Kyoto*

On the dirt road
back into town,
I passed a rice farm
as large as a city block.
A man stood
under the shade
of an umbrella pine, holding
a bottle of sake and a pear.
His right arm was covered
with the faded tattoo of a tiger.
I asked about his work,
and he told me
his aunt owned the farm,
and had given him a job
when he left jail.
He spends ten hours a day
bent over, putting rice slips
into the ground.
The work has ruined his back,
but he said he'd learned
more in that field
than he has anywhere else.
Gravity has humbled him.
When he plants rice,
he lowers his chest
and bows to the earth.

Waiting for Rain to Pass in Bashō's Hut
June 19, Bashō's hut

The sound of wind is replaced
by drops of water striking
tree branches. Spiders and moths
seek shelter beside my family
under Bashō's thatched roof.
The wooden walls have surrendered
to termites, birds, and the changing
of the seasons. The house has aged,
but the stones in front of Bashō's door
are smoother than they've ever been.

Riding the No. 5 to the Mountains
June 24, bus to Shisendo Temple

A monk stood
beside me on the bus
to Shisendo temple.
With one hand
he held the rail,
and with the other,
he waved a folding fan
to his face. He wore
wooden sandals,
a knee brace, aviators,
and a blue bandana.
Scars on his chest
peeked out
from his green robe.
We stepped off
at the same stop,
near the base
of the mountains.
I opened a map
while he crossed the street,
and walked into
a convenience store.

An Evening Before the Rain
June 24, Shisendo Temple: The Hall of Immortal Poets

Gnats fly over the garden
at the Hall of Immortal Poets.
Cicadas dig in the white sand,
and ants crawl over the patterns there.
The sand will need to be re-raked,
but the gardener doesn't mind.
His job, and the sacred grounds,
are timeless.

A Universal Accent
June 27, yakitori bar in Kyoto

I don't speak Japanese,
but I'm fluent in this yakitori bar.
I know how to order three
of whatever the person beside me is eating,
and three of the waitress's favorite.
I laugh with the guys at the bar,
and yell *kampai!* when we clink glasses.
We all sound the same
with our mouths filled with grilled meat.

Conversations by the Kamo River
July 1, by the Kamo River

A white-tailed hawk flies overhead, casting its shadow onto the river. The bird hasn't grown its white feathers yet; its body is still cloaked in black. My brother tells me about a time he felt depressed, and decided to travel for a change of pace. I never knew there was a time he was unhappy. I never thought of him as anything other than my brother. In front of us, the hawk dives into the water, and for a moment, disappears.

Daisen-In: The Academy of the Great Immortals
July 3, Daisen-In

I rub the arch of my foot
against the edge of the deck,
and look at the rock garden below.
My legs are stiff from walking all day,
and the wood is smooth—
Japanese Cypress grown beside the shrine.
The building has burned down
a dozen times, and has always
been rebuilt from the same grove of trees.
The stones in the garden
surrounding the temple
are arranged in lines,
circles and mounds.
Monks replace them
when they start to grow moss,
but the garden has been raked
in the same way, every morning,
for centuries.

The Home of Wild Animals
July 6, Imperial Palace southern pond

A man sits next to me on a rock,
and feeds turtles out of his hand.
Koi circle one another, and two cranes
eye the man from the roof of a shrine.
A stray cat sits beside me, licking itself.
When its fur is clean, it walks up
and brushes its head against my leg.
I reach down to pet it, and the cat hisses.
The man beside me says he comes every day
to make peace with the animals,
but he's never been able to approach the cat.
So it goes with stray animals, I say.
The cat is not lost, he replies,
it has made the world its home.

A Home to Rest In
July 7, recalling my first home in Kyoto

My home lies at the bottom
of the Higashiyama Mountains.
There, the June rain gives way
to low hanging clouds
that float among the trees.
A door in the bathroom
leads outside,
but doesn't fully open;
it's blocked by a stone wall
enclosing a small Buddhist shrine.
When I wash myself,
I keep the door ajar,
so the mirrors don't fog.
Every morning, steam
slips through the gap,
and disappears into the air
above the shrine.

A Crowd Around the Shrine
July 11, streets of Tokyo

Families used to line up
to pray at the small shrine
on Hankyu Street,
but now more people visit
the stores beside it:
a sneakers outlet,
and a fast food restaurant
that only serves to-go.
Thousands pass
this modest home of gods
without even noticing.
Staring at phones,
or the backs of heads,
the crowd stumbles
through the alley.
Fluorescent lights
shine at all hours,
and white noise
drowns out
the prayers of monks.

A Heron in the Garden
July 14, Kiyosumi Garden

I sat for hours on a bench at the Kiyosumi Garden,
and watched the fish swim aimlessly in a pond.
A great heron joined me, and stood by the edge
of the water. Patiently tracking the fish,
it kept its head fixed, and moved only its eyes.
It stood more still than its shadow,
which rippled on the surface of the pond. Suddenly,
it dipped its head into the water, and came up
with a large fish. The heron pointed
its beak to the sky, and massaged the meal
down its throat. Then it turned towards me,
as if to thank me for something I didn't know I'd done.

Where Owls Won't Fly
July 18, Tokyo

At night, grids of windows
shine from buildings
that stretch to the sky.
The streets glow
with cell phones, traffic lights,
and neon signs for drugstores
that never close. Street lamps
spill their light over the city
and brighten the pavement.
The stars are no longer visible,
and the city lights
lead nowhere.

Behind the Glass
July 20, Tokyo National Museum

The sword of the warlord Hideyoshi
lies on a podium behind a glass case.
The thick blade that cut the flesh
of dozens of bodies
has been polished and sharpened.
People crowd the exhibit
and take pictures, trying
to avoid their reflection in the glass.

Hunt
July 23, base of Mt. Hakone

The crows are eager to scavenge. Insatiable, they pick through trashcans, under trucks, on the roofs of buildings. They don't know what they're searching for, but they'll recognize it if they find it. They pass over dead rats and candy wrappers, and call to each other, *not here, not here.*

Poison
> *July 23, top of Mt. Hakone*

The fumes from Mt. Hakone
are stronger than they've been in years.
The air reeks of sulfur, the dirt
is stained a yellow-green,
and the trails have been blocked.
This has only brought more tourists.
People step past the caution tape
to get better photographs,
and pay locals to give them tours.
The locals smile when they explain
that breathing the gas can kill you.
The guides market death to remind the living
that they are only guests on this mountain.

Child's Play
> *July 27, Kakegawa*

Is your child out playing?
asks the women on the bench beside me.
I tell her, no, I came to the park alone.
She laughs, and says, enjoy it
while you can. As we talk,
her son climbs on her,
jumps onto her back,
leans over her shoulder,
and somersaults to the ground.
I used to play the same games
with my mother.
The woman falls silent,
and bounces her legs gently
while her son rests in her lap.

English Learning: Poetry
August 1, Ogaki

A notebook lies
on a stone bench in Ogaki,
soaked with rain.
The first half is full of equations
for water tension,
the speed of light, and gravity.
The rest of the pages
are filled with English phrases.
One section is titled,
"English Learning: Poetry,"
and has a list of vocab words:
autumn, persimmon, wind,
and the word *miracle* crossed out.

Aged Wine
August 8, Omihachiman

My neighbors pour
full glasses of wine,
and talk about sports,
new restaurants,
and the weather.
They don't realize
that nights like these
were dreamt of by poets,
and enjoyed by kings.
They pour another glass,
and say their kids
will have it good.
Someday surely,
their children
will say the same.

One More Mile
> *August 11, hiking trail behind Nanzen-ji Temple*

I keep walking, though my shirt
sticks to my chest, and the harsh sun burns.
Sweat falls from my forehead, arms, and legs,
and soaks my clothes. My breathing
is heavy, and with each step
it grows louder. I taste salt on my lips,
and I see through half-shut eyes.
My body feels as though it has melted,
and been forced back into shape.
This is why I keep walking.
It is the closest thing I have
to shedding my old body.

The Kamo River
August 12, banks of the Kamo River

A crane drops from the sky, and glides over the surface of the Kamo River. It follows the current downstream, beating its wings inches above the water. My mother always warned me to stay away from rivers like these. One wrong move and I could slip in, loose control, and drown. Now that I travel alone, I heed my mother's advice. I walk between the paved path and the water, just close enough to feel the mist on my face.

August

August 14, Uji

Poets of antiquity
drank themselves silly
on nights like these.
Fireflies glow,
and crickets sing
under a quarter moon—
a perfect excuse
for another drink.

Naked
August 15, Kyoto

In August, I bathe
in the outdoor shower
beside my cabin.
Hot water runs down my chest,
and my back feels stiff
against the evening air.
Steam rises from my body,
and drifts through the branches
of a Japanese cedar.
The familiar scent
of night-blooming jasmine,
carried on a soft breeze,
sweeps through the shower.
A white-cheeked starling
calls as he watches me
from above.
I'm rarely naked outdoors;
it's embarrassing
to feel so at home in the world.

No Other Life
August 17, Bashō's grave in Otsu

In the past three months, I have traveled
hundreds of miles, and bowed
to countless graves. I have walked
on dirt roads beaten down
by centuries of travelers, and I have admired
views painted by masters.
My hair has grown long, and my handwriting
looks more and more like my father's.
I still feel the same, but I know I've changed
because a year ago these words
could not have been written.
Now, all I hope is that
my thoughts amount to something,
like one man clapping in an audience,
or a heron that beats its wings once
to stay in the air just a while longer.

Cooper Young is a poet who hails from Santa Cruz, California, and currently studies in New Jersey. In 2018, Cooper was granted the Alex Adam Award through Princeton University to travel through Japan and write. Following the path of the famous poet, Matsuo Bashō, Cooper documented his journey through poetry and wrote this collection.

www.ingramcontent.com/pod-product-compliance
Lightning Source LLC
LaVergne TN
LVHW041520070426
835507LV00012B/1700